MW01503893

Sea Turtles

Contents

Text by Stanley L. Swartz
Photography by Robert Yin

DOMINIE PRESS
Pearson Learning Group

About Sea Turtles

Sea turtles live in the ocean. They have **flippers** for swimming. Some sea turtles weigh less than one pound. Others can be ten feet long and weigh almost two thousand pounds.

◀ Hawksbill Turtle

What Sea Turtles Eat

Sea turtles have no teeth. They have a hard edge on their **jaw**. This lets them eat animals like snails, fish, and crabs.

◄ Green Turtle

Sea turtles do not eat every day. They can go a whole month without eating. When food is **plentiful**, they eat more and grow big.

◀ Green Turtle

The Sea Turtle's Shell

Sea turtles have a hard outer shell. They can pull their head, flippers, and tail inside the shell. The shell **protects** them from their enemies. Some sea turtles live longer than humans.

◄ Green Turtle Sleeping on a Soft Coral Bed

How Sea Turtles Lay Their Eggs

Female sea turtles come ashore at night to lay their eggs. They come during high **tide**. It is hard for them to travel on land. They dig a hole in the sand for their eggs.

◀ **Female Green Turtle**

Sea turtles can lay up to 200 eggs.

The laid eggs are called a **clutch**.

Birds and small animals eat turtle eggs.

◀ Scientist Collects Turtle Eggs for a Project to Help Save Turtles

Baby Sea Turtles

The eggs **hatch** in several months. Baby sea turtles dig out of the sand. They hurry toward the water. Once they are in the water, they swim and are on their own.

◄ Baby Green Turtles

Older Sea Turtles

Sea turtles reach **maturity** in ten years. Scientists believe that sea turtles have a good sense of smell. Their eyes are also good, and they can see colors.

◄ Green Turtle at Maturity

Sea turtles do not make many sounds. When they are **mating**, they may grunt or bark. A few sea turtles can give a loud cry of anger.

◄ Two Green Turtles

Green Turtles

Green turtles can swim 250 miles in one week. Sea turtles have a good sense of location. They **migrate** every year.

◄ Green Turtle During Migration

Sea Turtles as Food

Some people eat turtle meat. Turtle eggs are also **prized** as food. Many types of sea turtles are endangered. We need to find ways to protect them.

◄ **Green Turtle**

Glossary

clutch:	A group of eggs
flipper:	A wide, flat limb used for swimming
hatch:	To break out of an egg
jaw:	Part of the mouth
mating:	Joined as a pair for breeding
maturity:	Fully grown
migrate:	To move from one place to another
plentiful:	A large amount
prized:	To value something highly
protect:	To keep from harm
tide:	The rise and fall of ocean water

Index